D1364999

WORLD WAR I WEAPONS

ESSENTIAL LIBRARY OF
WORLD WAR I

Essential Library

An Imprint of Abdo Publishing
abdopublishing.com

BY EMILY ROSE OACHS

CONTENT CONSULTANT

JUSTIN QUINN OLMSTEAD, PHD
ASSISTANT PROFESSOR OF HISTORY
UNIVERSITY OF CENTRAL OKLAHOMA

abdopublishing.com

Published by Abdo Publishing, a division of ABDO, PO Box 398166, Minneapolis, Minnesota 55439. Copyright © 2016 by Abdo Consulting Group, Inc. International copyrights reserved in all countries. No part of this book may be reproduced in any form without written permission from the publisher. Essential Library™ is a trademark and logo of Abdo Publishing.

Printed in the United States of America, North Mankato, Minnesota

092015
012016

Cover Photo: Everett Historical/Shutterstock Images
Interior Photos: Everett Historical/Shutterstock Images, 1, 14, 46, 49, 53, 57, 65, 74, 83, 85, 92, 96, 99 (top); John Warwick Brooke/Imperial War Museum, 4, 94; W. L. King, 8; London Illustrated London News and Sketch, 12; Red Line Editorial, 10; World History Archive/Newscom, 18; Public Domain, 22, 36; Robert B. Miller/Shutterstock Images, 24; Window & Grove, 17, 98 (left); Imperial War Museum, 26, 42; US Defense Visual Information Center, 30; Bettmann/Corbis, 32; Der Weltkrieg im Bild, 34; US Government, 39; Berliner Verlag/Archiv/DPA/Corbis, 45; Popular Science Monthly Volume 88, 55; Hulton-Deutsch Collection/ Corbis, 59; Stapleton Collection/Corbis, 60; Lebrecht Music & Arts/Corbis, 63; Mirrorpix/Newscom, 70; C. J. von Dühren/ General Services Administration/National Archives and Records Service/Office of the National Archives, 68; AP Images, 77, 80; US Marine Corps History Division, 86, 90, 98 (right), 99 (bottom)

Editor: Megan Anderson
Series Designers: Kelsey Oseid and Maggie Villaume

Library of Congress Control Number: 2015945650

Cataloging-in-Publication Data

Oachs, Emily Rose.
 World War I weapons / Emily Rose Oachs.
   p. cm. -- (Essential library of World War I)
 ISBN 978-1-62403-930-0 (lib. bdg.)
 Includes bibliographical references and index.
 1. World War, 1914-1918--Equipment and supplies--Juvenile literature. 2. Military weapons--History--20th century--Juvenile

CONTENTS

British soldiers rest in a German trench near the battalion's stranded Mark IV tank following the battle of Cambrai.

THE BATTLE OF CAMBRAI

A light mist shrouded the earth as dawn broke near Cambrai, France, on the morning of November 20, 1917. The silence and stillness of the morning stood in stark contrast to the violent, groundbreaking battle that was moments from starting.

A line of almost 400 British tanks stretched for nearly six miles (10 km).[1] These massive metal beasts stood hidden and camouflaged among the trees behind the British trenches. As daylight arrived, the tanks began moving. Lines of infantry followed behind. The colossal machines crawled across the gently rolling landscape. They advanced over the British line and into no-man's-land, heading directly for the German trenches.

The tanks cut commanding figures on the battlefield. These hulking armed and armored vehicles measured 26 feet (7.9 m) long and towered more than 8 feet (2.4 m) off the ground.[2] Their caterpillar tracks carried them easily over the uneven ground, and stripes of war paint camouflaged their metal bodies. Although they moved no more than four miles per hour (6.4 kmh), the tanks handily overcame German defenses. They attacked their enemies with machine-gun fire. Bullets pinged off their metal bodies. They crushed the nests of barbed wire littering no-man's-land. They uprooted trees standing in

THE GREAT WAR

World War I lasted from July 28, 1914, until November 11, 1918. The conflict started after the assassination of Austro-Hungarian Archduke Franz Ferdinand on June 28, 1914, in Sarajevo, Bosnia, by a member of a Serbian terrorist group. Ferdinand was heir to the Austro-Hungarian throne. Tensions between European countries were high even before, but his assassination led Austria-Hungary to declare war on Serbia, which appealed to its ally, Russia. As a result, Austria-Hungary's ally, Germany, declared war on Russia on August 1, 1914. The two sides of the war were the Central powers and the Allies. Germany and Austria-Hungary formed the Central powers, while the United Kingdom, France, and Russia made up the Allies. When the United States entered the war in 1917, it joined the Allies. Fighting took place on the eastern and western fronts. Stretching north to south from the Baltic Sea to the Black Sea, the eastern front included fighting in most of Eastern Europe and spread into Central Europe. The western front stretched from the English Channel to the Swiss border.

their paths. They even drove over wide German trenches, using heavy bundles of brushwood as makeshift bridges.

At 6:20 a.m., the British opened fire on the unsuspecting German line, bombarding them with machine guns, shells, and explosives. As one British tank officer described, "The whole of the enemy's lines were lit up in a tossing bubbling torrent of multicolored flame."[3]

NO-MAN'S-LAND

No-man's-land was the desolate, neutral ground between the lines of the Allies and the Central powers. Exploded shells and gunfire scarred this dangerous stretch of land. Soldiers attempting to charge the enemy had to cross through no-man's-land. This left them vulnerable to gunfire from enemies, who were protected by their trenches. As a result, bodies of dead soldiers from both armies were strewn across the ground, unburied.

A hail of German machine-gun fire and trench mortars fell around the tanks in response. But the tanks' armored bodies were bulletproof against machine-gun fire, and no obstacle seemed difficult for the tanks to overcome. A German officer later recounted his chilling encounter with the British tanks at Cambrai: "I could see a whole chain of these steel monsters advancing toward our trenches. The tank to our front was barely a hundred meters [330 feet] away by now. The light machine gun had fired off its last belt of ammunition without visible effect. What was to be done?"[4]

The German soldiers were left apparently defenseless against the new British weapon. They could only watch as the war machines continued their slow, measured advance toward their trenches.

The desolation of no-man's-land reflected the war's destruction.

The battle of Cambrai was not the first time German troops had seen tanks in battle. It was, however, the first time tanks were mobilized en masse. Cambrai showed the true potential of these battlefield tanks for the first time. The British had developed the tanks to fill a specific need on the battlefield. They needed these armored war machines to help break the deadlock that had grown on the western front.

THE TRENCHES OF WORLD WAR I

By 1915, the Germans of the Central powers and the British and French of the Allies had fought themselves into a stalemate. Both sides underestimated the power of modern, automatic weapons. Machine guns, rapid-firing artillery, and magazine-fed rifles had already seen battle in the Boer War (1899–1902) and the Russo-Japanese War (1904–05). But nobody predicted just how lethal and destructive the weapons could be. Military officers on both sides attempted to combat these modern weapons using freshly outdated military tactics.

At the war's start, military officials employed the same tactics they had used successfully in wars of the past. They held that the key to success was to attack first. So officers sent masses of infantry charging forward. But foot charges were no match for automatic weapons, nor were strategies that called for mass formations. However, officers continued using their obsolete strategies, even after they were proven ineffective. Soldiers were still sent to charge the enemy with rifle and bayonet, only to be mowed down by enemy fire. One British officer observed, "[The French officers] advance about 20 yards [18 m] ahead of their men as calmly as though on parade, but so far I have not seen one of them get more than 50 yards [46 m] without being knocked over."[5] On the battlefield, there was nowhere to take cover. Advancing men were exposed and vulnerable targets for the enemy, who were able to take aim from the protection of their trenches.

Continued use of these strategies resulted in a deadlock on the western front. It prompted both sides to dig into the ground for protection. Armies carved vast trenches into the landscape. They used the trenches as shelter and defense against enemy fire. In total, a maze of approximately 25,000 miles (40,000 km) of trenches was constructed. They stretched 470 miles (760 km)

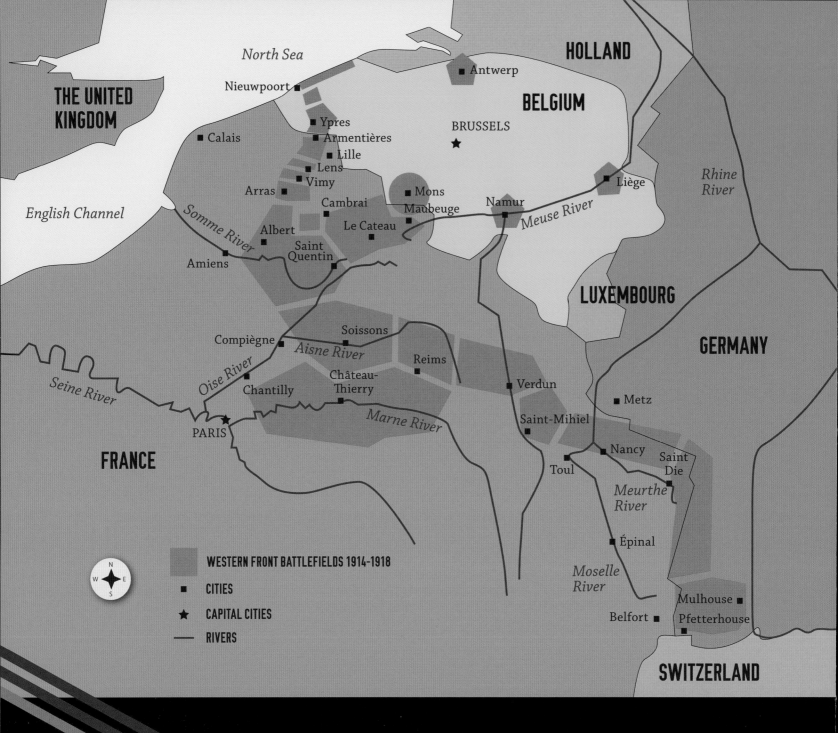

The western front

along the western front, from the English Channel to the Swiss border.[6] Once their positions were in place, the lines moved little—at most ten miles (16 km) in either direction—over the next three and a half years.

BREAKING THE DEADLOCK

Breaking the deadlock required innovation. The Germans and the French and British had arranged secure defenses for themselves. Their trench systems grew elaborate and wide. They arranged barbed wire in no-man's-land to hold back attacking soldiers. They built fortifications for their weapons, which protected their gunmen as they fired on the enemy. These defenses were particular to trench warfare. And they were difficult to beat with the weapons of the past. Both sides would have to work to create new weapons and refine old ones to suit the needs of the trenches.

British colonel Ernest Dunlop Swinton saw the unique problem trenches presented. He recognized that the British needed a weapon designed specifically

BATTLEFIELD BRAVERY

When the Great War began, the French army trusted that its troops could overcome any obstacle using spirit and bravery. The troops quickly learned, however, that battlefield bravery did not matter when they were faced with automatic weapons. Future French president Charles de Gaulle experienced this firsthand during the war. As he described it,

With affected calm, the officers let themselves be killed standing upright, some obstinate platoons stuck their bayonets in their rifles, bugles sounded the charge . . . but all to no purpose. In an instant it had become clear that not all the courage in the world could withstand this fire.[7]

to beat defenses in the trenches. So he suggested creating "some moving bulletproof device which could not only climb forward and forge its way through uncut wire, but could knock out machine-guns in a straight fight."[8] The vehicle he described would eventually become the tank.

Other weapons, too, were invented or improved out of necessity. Weapons that had been popularly employed in the 1700s were reimagined to suit the needs of the trenches. This resulted in modern grenades and trench mortars. Airplanes were originally used for aerial observation and eventually were armed with machine guns. Zeppelins, or airships, were invented in 1900. During the war,

Both sides, including these French soldiers, were forced to dig in and live in a maze of trenches.

CONDITIONS IN THE ALLIED TRENCHES

Life in the Allied trenches was far from pleasant for soldiers. Standing water filled the bottoms of the muddy trenches, and temperatures were cold. As one British soldier remembered, "When you take your boots off, [your feet are] like a washerwoman's hands, all wrinkled, cold and everything was shrunken, terrible."[10] Day after day of standing in these conditions resulted in painful swelling of the feet, or "trench foot." Some cases were so extreme that soldiers suffered gangrene or needed to have a foot amputated. The British military alone treated 20,000 soldiers for trench foot during the winter of 1914–1915.[11]

The trenches were also home to the bodies of dead soldiers, and the stench of their decaying bodies filled the trenches. One British soldier described how soldiers' bones poked through the trench walls, "and skulls appeared like mushrooms." He described, too, that in the trenches he once "found a pair of boots, still containing someone's feet."[12]

Germany used them to drop bombs on cities. Both the Germans and the Allies experimented with the use of poisonous gas to attack unsuspecting opponents. And in 1915, the Germans introduced the flamethrower, a new weapon capable of spraying liquid fire up to 20 yards (18 m).

Technological advances completely altered the way World War I was conducted. Necessity demanded both sides develop new weapons to prevent mass slaughter. Historian Libby O'Connell said of the advancements during World War I, "Soldiers rode in on horses, and they left in airplanes."[9]

The evolution of the machine gun during World War I changed combat.

MODERN WEAPONS

The war's first trenches emerged after the first battle of the Marne in September 1914. German soldiers dug themselves into position atop a ridge, and the Allies followed suit two days later, carving their own trenches to directly face the German army. By late October, more trenches were dug along the front, setting the stage for the stalemate and carnage of the next four years.

MACHINE GUNS

Neither side was prepared for the devastating effectiveness of machine guns in battle. Their overbearing might demanded soldiers dig into the ground and build fortifications, such as pillboxes, for protection and escape.

Hiram Maxim built the first machine gun in approximately 1884. This early version already proved to be a formidable weapon, firing up to 700 rounds per minute (RPM). During World War I, trained marksmen could fire at most 15 RPM from rifles fed by magazines, or ammunition storage and feeding devices attached to a firearm.[1] The machine gun's speed came from its ability to reload using the energy created from firing the previous bullet, rather than reloading by hand. Before the machine gun, soldiers had to use a crank or lever to perform this operation themselves. The single barrel of a Maxim machine gun was also surrounded by a water jacket, designed to prevent the gun from overheating. After Maxim's first machine gun, other people began designing and manufacturing machine guns as well.

Early in the war, machine guns were largely immobile. They were heavy weapons, weighing up to 70 pounds (32 kg), and they were mounted on tripods.[2] Teams of soldiers were needed to wield a single machine gun. However, they had the ability to fire approximately 550 RPM and could shoot up to 600 yards (550 m).[3]

PILLBOXES

German pillboxes were fortified positions for machine guns. Built of concrete, these structures protected machine gunners from enemy fire. A small slot on the front of a pillbox enabled gunners to shoot at the enemy while making it more difficult for the enemy to hit them. Pillboxes were strategically placed along the line. Should the enemy attempt to attack a pillbox from close quarters, the enemy was vulnerable to fire from other pillboxes.

HIRAM MAXIM

1840–1916

Born in 1840 in Maine, Hiram Maxim showed an early ability for invention. In 1866, at 26, he secured his first patent for a hair curling iron. By the 1870s, Maxim worked at the United States Electric Lighting Company. There he invented the carbon filaments used in electric light bulbs.

Maxim relocated to London, England, in 1881. In 1883, a friend reportedly told Maxim, "Hang your electricity. If you want to make your fortune, invent something to help these fool Europeans kill each other more quickly!"[4] He developed the first automatic gun in 1884. Germany, Russia, Austria, Hungary, Switzerland, and the United Kingdom quickly adopted Maxim's machine gun. It was also the primary gun used by Germany and Russia throughout World War I.

Later, Maxim became interested in aviation. In 1891, he developed a steam-powered airplane. The airplane managed to take flight briefly before crashing and becoming damaged. By the end of his life, in 1916, Maxim had obtained 271 patents.

British soldiers use the Vickers machine gun during the first battle of the Somme in 1916.

Originally the British used the Maxim gun, but they switched to the Vickers machine gun in 1912. They eventually changed guns again, transitioning to the Lewis machine gun. The Lewis gun was lighter and more mobile than the Vickers. However, it still required a team of soldiers to operate. Six men were required for each Lewis machine gun. One man, the most experienced, shot the gun. A second man carried spare parts, while the other four carried ammunition.

As the war progressed, smaller machine guns—called light machine guns—were developed. These weighed up to 28 pounds (13 kg) and could be manned by a single soldier.

MACHINE GUNS ON THE BATTLEFIELD

Machine guns dominated the battlefield, capable of obliterating the enemy. One soldier remembered his encounter with enemy machine guns: "Men began to stumble and fall, then to go down like standing corn before a scythe."[5] Where the machine guns led, mass carnage followed. Even if outnumbered, soldiers could hold back their enemy using machine guns. No number of troops could defeat an enemy that held superior weapons. On the first day of the first battle of the Somme in Picardy, France, in July 1916, the British amassed 100,000 troops. Marching shoulder to shoulder, the soldiers advanced toward the German lines. Approximately 100 German machine guns inflicted 60,000 British casualties, 19,000 of which resulted in death.[6]

Mass formations, relics of a different era of war, proved particularly easy to defeat. About the battle of Loos, which lasted from September 25 to October 13, 1915, the diary of the Fifteenth German Reserve Regiment recorded,

> *Ten columns of extended line could clearly be distinguished, each one estimated at more than a thousand men, and offering such a target as had never been seen before, or even thought possible. Never had the machine gunners had such straightforward work to do nor done it so effectively.*[7]

Lines of soldiers offered clear targets for machine guns. With the speed and power of the weapons, soldiers could handily mow down men congregated in one area. As the Fifteenth Reserve Regiment went on to describe, "[The soldiers] could be seen falling literally in hundreds."[8] Of the 10,000 men involved in this attack, more than 8,000 soldiers and officers suffered casualties.[9]

ARTILLERY

The immense value of artillery, or large-caliber guns, became clear once soldiers had settled into the trenches. Both sides used artillery to prepare the battlefield for an advance. These preparations were called barrages, or concentrated artillery attacks. They aimed at eroding the enemy's defenses before battle began. Artillery gunners would unleash what they called hurricane bombardments in preparation for an infantry advance. These were short barrages that preceded attacks.

Other barrages were far longer, preceding attacks by a few days. Before the first battle of the Somme, a five-day-long bombardment ended with 224,221 shells dropped in the hour before the battle started.[10] A German soldier observed,

> A storm of artillery broke with a crash along the entire line. . . . All around there was howling, snarling and hissing. With a sharp ringing sound, the death-dealing shells burst, spewing their leaden fragments against our line.[11]

So powerful was this particular barrage that the explosions were heard in London, England, approximately 140 miles (230 km) away. Some gunners reported bleeding ears after hearing the five days of unceasing bombardment prior to the battle.

The United Kingdom was the first to utilize artillery in a strategy that came to be known as the creeping barrage. The creeping barrage was, in effect, a curtain formed by artillery shells dropping into no-man's-land. These shells slowly progressed forward with the movement of British infantry. This protected soldiers from enemy fire as they advanced across no-man's-land toward enemy lines.

Different types of artillery shells achieved different desired results. Hundreds of small lead balls filled shrapnel shells. These shells had timed explosions. They would detonate over enemy lines, showering unprotected soldiers with a hail of metal pellets. Other shells were filled with highly explosive materials. When they landed, the shells would explode. No-man's-land has been described as a "lunar landscape" because of the craters formed from exploding shell blasts.[12] Artillery gunners used these explosive

PARIS GUN

On March 23, 1918, a series of explosions rattled Paris. Allied commanders soon realized that the explosions came from projectiles shot from massive artillery guns. These huge guns were located behind Germany's lines—approximately 75 miles (120 km) away.[13]

The gun itself was 128 feet (39 m) long, and its explosive-filled artillery shell weighed up to 278 pounds (126 kg). The gun launched the shell at a speed of 5,407 feet per second (1,648 mps).[14] The shell soared through the atmosphere, reaching a peak altitude of 24 miles (39 km).[15] Germany's seven so-called Kaiser Wilhelm guns shelled Paris off and on for four months.

An Austro-Hungarian siege howitzer in 1914

shells to destroy trenches, while larger siege guns were used to break through reinforced defenses and fortresses.

Among the artillery used were howitzers. These large, deadly artillery guns could shoot projectiles both on a flat plane like a cannon, or at an arc, like a mortar. "Big Bertha" was the nickname given to Germany's massive 16.5-inch (41.9 cm) howitzer, the largest to be used in the war. Weighing 47 short tons (43 metric tons) itself, this gargantuan howitzer could launch a 1,785-pound

(810 kg) shell up to six miles (10 km).[16] Germany first employed these artillery pieces in 1914, against Belgium's reinforced forts around Liège. A total of 12 of the Big Bertha howitzers were built and used during World War I.

HELMETS

Soldiers entered into World War I without any real protection for their heads. British troops wore soft fabric caps, while German soldiers wore leather helmets that offered little protection from flying shrapnel.

In previous wars, the soft helmets provided all the protection soldiers needed. But by 1915, it became clear soldiers needed better helmets. In World War I, soldiers on western front battlefields no longer faced fire solely from the front.

Fire also came at them from above. Shrapnel and other dangerous flying debris increased the number of casualties from head wounds.

The French were the first to introduce hard helmets, in July 1915. The British Brodie helmet debuted with a limited run in 1915, and mass production

FLAMETHROWER

When Germany introduced its *flammenwerfer*, or flamethrower, in 1915, the new weapon terrified Allied troops. One British officer described their effects as being "like a line of powerful fire-hoses spraying fire instead of water across my fire-trench."[17]

These intimidating new weapons used canisters of nitrogen to spray a thick liquid petroleum mixture from their hoses. An igniter transformed the liquid into a stream of flames and lit the mixture. One soldier carried Germany's backpack version, while another aimed and operated it.

German soldiers wore steel helmets such as this one during World War I.

began in 1916. Germany followed with its *Stahlhelm*, or "steel helmet," design in early 1916. Since then, hard metal helmets have been recognized as important equipment for soldiers, and they are still a part of soldiers' uniforms today.

THE MIGHT OF ARTILLERY AND MACHINE GUNS

The immense power of machine guns and artillery during the war is undeniable. The rapid increase in artillery holdings reflected its usefulness on the battlefield.

France entered the war with approximately 3,000 artillery pieces. By the end of the war, its artillery contained more than 12,500 pieces. Germany, too, saw a vast increase in its artillery holdings, which more than doubled to 17,455 pieces in 1917. Italy's pieces of artillery increased by nearly four times throughout the war; from 1915 through 1918, Italy's artillery supplies skyrocketed from 2,121 pieces to 7,995.[18]

As they had with artillery, commanders entered the war with far fewer machine guns than they would ultimately need. Allied armies, in particular, vastly underestimated machine guns' power in battle. Prior to the war, the British military believed each battalion required just two machine guns. But trench warfare forced the military to increase each battalion's number sixteenfold. After the war, in 1919, the United States upped this number to 336 machine guns for each regiment.[19]

Artillery fire caused up to 70 percent of deaths on the battlefield.[20] Machine gun and rifle fire were responsible for claiming 39 percent of British Expeditionary Forces. Machine guns and artillery were the conflict's greatest killers.[21] Their presence turned the battlefields of World War I into a bloodbath.

WEAPONS IN THE TRENCHES

Although not as dominant as machine guns, rifles too played an important role in battle. Each soldier was issued a rifle and bayonet upon entering the war. Rifles allowed soldiers to move around quickly in battle. Weighing approximately nine pounds (4 kg), rifles were considerably more mobile than heavy artillery and machine guns. Soldiers could easily haul these weapons and their ammunition onto the battlefield with them.

RIFLES AND BAYONETS

Almost all rifles had magazines, which stored and fed ammunition to the device. In the hands of trained marksmen, these rifles could also have an impact similar to that of machine guns. At Mons in 1914, experienced British riflemen were able to shoot 15 RPM, striking targets some 1,000 yards (900 m) away.[1] Thousands of Germans fell to the fire, and British riflemen were so precise the Germans believed they had come under machine-gun fire.

LANCE AND SABER

Early in the war, an elite squadron of German cavalrymen was destroyed at the battle of Haelen on August 12, 1914. The German soldiers rode horses and were armed with lances and sabers, traditional cavalry armaments. They continually charged a line of Belgian soldiers. But the lances and sabers were no match for the Belgians' rifles. The German cavalrymen were slaughtered in the gunfire.

Russia faced a dire rifle shortage in 1915. At one point, the Russian military asked France for 1.5 million rifles because they could not produce enough to arm their soldiers at the front.[2] Rifles were so scarce that, according to the Russian chief of staff, in some regiments, "These poor devils [soldiers] had to wait patiently under a shower of shrapnel until their comrades fell before their eyes and they could pick up their arms."[3] German soldiers even captured Russian soldiers who were equipped only with clubs as they waited for more of their comrades to die, at which point they could take their rifles.

Snipers used rifles to target unwitting soldiers who accidentally exposed their heads to the enemy. Colonel Swinton explained, "Woe betide the man who in daylight puts up his head carelessly to take a long glance at [no-man's-land]."[4]

Any man who allowed his head to show above the trench was at risk of becoming the next victim of an expert marksman.

While soldiers were given bayonets, the war proved them largely obsolete. A bayonet was a blade that could be attached to the end of a rifle. Bayonet charges had once been successful in battle. But in World War I, attempts to lead bayonet charges often led to mass slaughter of the soldiers. Protected by the trenches, machine guns could easily cut down advancing soldiers before they came near enough to use the bayonet.

Bayonets were, however, useful at times in close quarters in the trenches. During a May 1916 battle, a handful of Ottoman soldiers managed to survive the gunfire and break into the trenches of Australians and New Zealanders. These lucky few, however, were brought down by bayonets.

OBSERVATION TREES

The British built fake trees to serve as observation points for snipers. Soldiers would photograph, measure, and sketch dead trees on the battlefield. The military sent those images to artists, who would then re-create the dead trees. Inside, they included scaffolding to allow a sniper or observer to climb the tower. When the fake tree was complete, it would be shipped to the front. Hidden by darkness, soldiers would remove the real tree and "plant" the fake tree in its place. By morning, the swap would be complete, and British snipers had a camouflaged lookout in the middle of the battlefield.

Two US soldiers practice using a bayonet.

TRENCH RAIDS

Masked by the cloak of night, 100 Canadian soldiers launched a surprise attack against German trenches on February 28, 1915. Five of the Canadians were killed in the raid, and another ten were wounded, but the soldiers were successful in devastating 30 yards (27 m) of German trenches.

Canadian troops continued conducting these stealthy raids until late in 1916. The raids were used to collect information, attack the enemy, and capture prisoners to interrogate. Other belligerents, such as Germany and France, also took up the practice. These high-risk endeavors often resulted in many casualties on both sides.

As trench raids continued, soldiers required weapons designed specifically for these operations. As they crawled toward the enemy, their rifles and bayonets were too difficult to handle. The troops could not easily sneak their way to enemy trenches with such awkward rifles, and the bayonet blades were too long to be easily and effectively used at close range. On raiding missions, therefore, soldiers traded in their bayonets for shorter trench knives. They also often used grenades and lightweight machine guns during raids.

GEAR

Upon entering World War I, most soldiers in the British infantry carried approximately 45 pounds (20 kg) of gear, supplies, and weapons such as bayonets and rifles. Officers typically carried pistols. Just as the methods of warfare changed, the supplies soldiers needed to carry changed as well. As the war progressed, soldiers added hard metal helmets, varying types of gas masks, and often grenades, extra ammunition, and trench knives to their load. By 1916, some soldiers carried up to 75 pounds (34 kg) of supplies.

Raiding soldiers also carried with them effective unofficial, homemade weapons, such as trench clubs. One soldier described seeing a particularly lethal club, called a knobkerrie, used. He observed, "They were nasty looking things,"

with nails protruding from one end.[5] Soldiers on trench raids would throw a grenade into an enemy's dugout. If anyone survived the bomb, the soldiers would strike the fleeing enemy with their clubs.

BARBED WIRE

Among the war's most effective defensive weapons was barbed wire. Soldiers stretched massive tangles of barbed wire across no-man's-land. Wooden or iron stakes driven into the ground held the wire in place. These barriers sometimes reached three to five feet (0.9 to 1.5 m) high and extended for 30 yards (27 m) deep.[6]

BINOCULARS

Snipers were a real danger to those in the trenches. So great was the risk that soldiers began to use special binoculars to survey no-man's-land. These binoculars were similar to periscopes. The lenses looked out over the parapet. This enabled soldiers to safely gaze through them without becoming a target for waiting enemy snipers.

Both sides arranged the wire in front of their trenches to protect themselves from the enemy. As infantry charged, soldiers often became entangled in the enemy's wire. Unable to free themselves, they fell victim to enemy fire. One soldier described the barbed wire in no-man's-land the morning after a battle:

> *Hundreds of dead . . . were strung like wreckage washed up on a high-water mark. Quite as many had died on the enemy wire as on the ground, like fish caught in a net. They hung there in grotesque postures.*[7]

Fellow soldiers would be shot if they tried to help their fallen comrades.

Coils of barbed wire surrounded trenches and were used to steer the enemy into

Sometimes soldiers built mazes from the wire. These were designed to corral enemy soldiers into specific areas. Machine guns would be trained on those killing zones, ready to shoot the enemy if they were herded within range.

Barbed wire was difficult to defeat. Cutting it with wire cutters proved nearly impossible when under attack. Exploding shells often had little effect on the wire. The barbed wire only became more tangled as the shells blew it into the air. The wire's coils absorbed the energy of the blast. In time, troops solved the barbed wire problem using chicken wire. Tossing rolls of chicken wire over the barbed wire created a kind of bridge, enabling soldiers to crawl over the barrier. American soldiers also developed Bangalore torpedoes—metal cylinders filled with dynamite. Soldiers shoved them under the barbed wire, exploding an opening in the barrier.

Austro-Hungarian soldiers throw grenades from the trenches

WEAPONS OF SIEGE WARFARE

World War I was a period of great technological innovation. Many weapons used during the war had never been seen before. But some of the most useful weapons on the western front were taken straight from the past. Many weapons developed for medieval warfare were used alongside the ultramodern machine guns and tanks on the battlefield.

SIEGE WARFARE AND THE TRENCHES

As the belligerents settled into the trenches on the western front, the style of warfare that developed was very similar to the siege warfare of past centuries. In both siege warfare and trench warfare, soldiers were shielded by strong defenses. The trenches made it difficult for the enemy to fire directly at soldiers. During World War I, machine guns and rifles were not as effective. These weapons could only fire directly onto the enemy. Instead, soldiers needed weapons that could be launched into the trenches. Both sides took old siege warfare weapons such as grenades and mortars and adapted them for use in the trenches.

TRENCH MORTAR

Mortars were introduced in 1673. They were used for siege warfare during World War I. They were short-range artillery guns ranging in size from light to heavy. They were short tubes that launched explosive shells at steep inclines high into the air. The shells arced through the air for a few hundred yards before dropping behind enemy defenses.

When the war began, Germany had approximately 150 trench mortars. It planned to use them to barrage ridges surrounding its forts in the Moselle region of France. However, by the end of 1914, Germany had also installed these mortars in its trenches, a few hundred yards away from enemy trenches. These mortars would destroy any defenses the Allies constructed. Germany's mortars were also highly mobile. This enabled Germany to stealthily gather 835 trench mortars along a 12.5-mile (20 km) stretch in preparation for an offensive in March 1918.[1]

Some trench mortars were stationary weapons.

The Allies responded with mortars of their own. They took mortar designs from previous war models. France's first mortar arrived at the western front in April 1915. In contrast to German mortars, Allied mortars tended to be far less mobile. It took until 1918 for the Allies to introduce a mortar sufficiently mobile for combat.

Italy developed the largest trench mortar of the war. This massive weapon weighed 25,700 pounds (11,700 kg). Its shells weighed 580 pounds (260 kg), which could be launched 4,470 yards (4,090 m).[2]

GRENADES

Grenades were small, handheld bombs first used in the 1400s. Soldiers would toss them into crowds of enemy soldiers gathered outside fortresses under attack. Around 1750, they fell into disuse.

But during World War I, the specific conditions of trench warfare resulted in a widespread renewal of their use. Grenades were useful for attacking enemy soldiers in their trenches. Soldiers throwing grenades would have to approach within 30 yards (27 m) of an enemy trench. Some British soldiers entered the war carrying basic grenades. But in 1914, soldiers typically made their own grenades. They would fill empty jam tins with nails and other scrap metal, and then pack them tight with gunpowder. However, these handmade weapons often exploded too soon, injuring their makers as often as their enemy targets.

In 1915, Germany unleashed its first mass-produced grenade, the stick bomb. Explosives were attached to one end of a handle, which enabled soldiers to effortlessly hurl the grenades. These stick bombs were easy to throw, with a range of approximately 44 yards (40 m). However, they produced smaller explosions than other grenades. In response, the United Kingdom released its egg-shaped Mills bomb. It generated larger explosions than Germany's grenades but could be thrown only 30 yards (27 m).[3]

Grenades rapidly became an important weapon for soldiers. Eventually all infantrymen carried grenades with them. As the war progressed, both sides also developed new grenades that could release chemical gas or ignite fires.

MILLS BOMB

First introduced in 1915, the British Mills bomb became the most widely used hand grenade. The round grenades resembled pineapples, with lines carved into their surface. Before throwing a Mills bomb, soldiers had to remove a pin from the grenade. The pin released a trigger that lit the bomb's fuse. Soldiers had approximately seven seconds to throw the grenade before it would explode. By 1917, the United Kingdom was producing approximately 1 million Mills bombs each week.

UNDERGROUND MINING AND THE BATTLE OF MESSINES

A common strategy used in traditional siege warfare was underground mining. Men would dig tunnels under enemy walls and fortifications, plant mines, and detonate them to collapse the enemy's fortifications.

The British mass-produced the Mills bombs for use in combat during World War I.

Both sides used this medieval technique on western front battlefields as well. Sappers dug under important strategic points along the enemy's line and installed explosives, hoping to blow up the enemy. Underground mining reached its peak in 1916. During this period, the British unleashed 750 mines along the front, and Germany detonated approximately the same amount as well.[4]

Underground mining was dangerous work. Tunnels were in constant danger of collapsing and could fill at any moment with deadly carbon monoxide gas from shells and rifle bullets. Also, the explosive mines sappers planted could unexpectedly detonate at any time.

GEOPHONE

To listen for enemy tunnelers, a French scientist developed the geophone. This device enabled soldiers to magnify—by two and a half times—the sound of people tunneling. The geophone was designed like a stethoscope with two discs at the end. Listeners placed the two discs against either the floor or wall of a tunnel. Using the geophone, trained listeners could estimate enemy tunnels' depth and distance from the listener.

Sappers also often had to work in silence. Soldiers listened underground for the sound of enemy sappers to hear miners' voices or their shovels as they dug. If miners were discovered, soldiers aboveground would plant explosives to try to cause the enemy's tunnels to collapse. Sometimes sappers would encounter enemy tunnels, or accidentally dig directly into enemy trenches. Underground battles followed these accidental encounters. To compensate for the dangerous nature of their job, sappers were paid four times more than regular soldiers.

MINERS

Battlefield tunnels were very cramped, claustrophobic spaces. They could be just two feet (0.6 m) wide and four feet (1.2 m) high. The miners often had to bend over double to walk through the dark tunnels, and it was difficult for two miners to pass each other in the tight space.

Most tunnelers in World War I had been miners before the war. Many had not initially been accepted into the military because of their age or health. But their earlier years of mining experience prepared them for the unique work of the tunneling companies.

Armies often used these mining tactics with other offensives or raids. The Allies notably employed this strategy at the battle of Messines in 1917. The German military held the Messines Ridge in western Belgium, and the British needed to take control of the area. Starting in 1915, the British army made preparations to overtake the ridge. It dug a system of deep explosive-filled tunnels that ran under the ridge. Some tunnels were 100 feet (30 m) deep and stretched for 2,000 feet (610 m).[5]

To begin the battle, the British artillery bombarded the German line for four days. Early in the morning of June 7, 1916, the explosives were detonated. Almost simultaneously, 19 mines erupted from below the ground.[6] Immediately following the explosion, artillery added fire to the battlefield.

The blasts created enormous craters—some as large as 260 feet (80 m) across. The explosions could be heard in London, 140 miles (225 km) away. Approximately 10,000 German soldiers died immediately after the mines exploded.[7] By the day's end, the British had won the battle of Messines.

Mines were buried and positioned to keep the enemy from advancing.

After Messines, underground mining was no longer used. The pace of the war picked up and neither side had the time to carve explosive-laden shafts into the earth.

German U-boats were underwater threats to the Allies.

U-BOATS

Early on a Tuesday morning, September 22, 1914, a U-boat submarine caught sight of three British cruisers. The *Aboukir*, the *Hogue*, and the *Cressy* were patrolling the waters near the Dutch coast. The U-boat quickly submerged and moved into torpedo range. German lieutenant Otto Weddigen took aim at the middle ship. He released his torpedo, and it sailed through the water, striking the *Aboukir* just under its magazine. The ammunition exploded and a burst of fire flared from the ship.

To the crew on the ship, the enemy was invisible. The other two ships came to rescue the *Aboukir*'s sinking sailors. Another torpedo struck the *Hogue*, which was seriously damaged. Weddigen observed, "For twenty minutes the *Hogue* lay wounded and helpless on the surface before she heaved, half turned over, and sank."[1]

Just one ship remained: the *Cressy*. Underwater, the U-boat crept into position and fired two torpedoes. Both struck, and the ship tilted far to its side. Weddigen noted that after an explosion on the ship, "she sank with a loud sound, as if from a creature in pain."[2]

Three ships were sunk, and 1,459 men died in less than an hour.[3] The cause was hidden under the waves. Prior to World War I, submarines were untested as offensive weapons. But after one German U-boat sank these three British cruisers, the new weapons proved their stealthy advantage.

UNDERWATER MENACE

U-boat came from the German word *Unterseeboot*, or "undersea boat." Of all the belligerents, Germany used its U-boats most effectively during World War I. Germany's submarines were generally approximately 215 feet (65 m) long and carried 35 crew members. Diesel engines ran the U-boats at the ocean's surface, but once submerged, electric motors run by batteries supplied power. Battery life limited submarines' ability to stay submerged, so they spent the vast majority of their time at the ocean's surface. Most could stay underwater for approximately two hours. Each vessel had a periscope, which enabled the crew to see above the ocean's surface.

Torpedoes made U-boats formidable opponents. Later in the war, U-boats had four torpedo tubes and carried 12 torpedoes. Torpedoes were virtually

Allied sailors escape via lifeboats after a German torpedo struck their ship.

submarines themselves, equipped with their own engines and rudders. Reaching 20 feet (6 m) in length, they could travel four miles (6.4 km) to reach their targets. With torpedoes, U-boats could launch surprise attacks, approaching targets undetected and striking them with 500-pound (230 kg) warheads. Targeted ships had almost no defense against torpedo attacks.

Along with torpedoes, U-boats were equipped with deck guns. These guns proved an effective, relatively inexpensive way to take out enemy ships. U-boats would rise to the surface to open fire on targets. The U-boats were exposed whenever they surfaced, and men had to be on deck to operate these guns. These guns were part of normal cruiser warfare, which was considered legitimate compared with unrestricted submarine warfare.

UNDERWATER MINES

Just as submarines attacked unseen, underwater mines were invisible ocean predators. These globe-shaped mines were filled with explosives and had spokes sticking out at the top that were part of the detonation mechanism. They floated below the water's surface, with cables anchoring them to the ocean floor. If a ship made contact with a mine, it would explode. Mines were effective weapons, responsible for sinking almost 3 million short tons (2.7 million metric tons) of cargo.[4]

The British naval fleet patrolled the North Sea, laying mines and cutting off access. This prevented supplies such as raw materials and food from reaching Germany. Author and historian Richard Hough described the North Sea as "a marine no man's land, with the British Fleet bottling up the exits."[5]

Germany developed U-boats whose purpose was specifically to plant mines in the ocean. Laying mines proved to be a dangerous task. Many U-boat crews and vessels were lost during the process. Either the mines would explode prematurely, or the U-boat itself would accidentally strike other mines already positioned.

UNRESTRICTED SUBMARINE WARFARE

For centuries, the British Royal Navy was the most powerful in the world. At the war's onset, the British navy began an illegal blockade on German ports. Fearing U-boat attacks, the Royal Navy stopped ships at a distance in the North Sea and prevented them from entering German harbors, or other neutral ports. This prevented German troops from receiving important food and supplies. German civilians were also denied much-needed food and other materials.

Germany's navy did not have nearly the power of the United Kingdom's. To counter the blockade, Germany announced on February 4, 1915, it would pursue unrestricted submarine warfare. Any ships—neutral or enemy, merchant or military—spotted in a war zone were subject to attack without warning. U-boats were free to strike without surfacing. They could torpedo and sink a ship without revealing themselves to the enemy.

A German U-boat attack sank the British passenger liner *Lusitania* on May 7, 1915, killing 1,195 of its passengers.[6] Public outcry in the United Kingdom, France, and the United States compelled Germany to agree to leave passenger liners alone. By September, Germany's U-boat fleet halted its unrestricted warfare. But in those five months, German submarines had managed to sink more than 450 ships.[7]

LUSITANIA

The RMS *Lusitania* became a high-profile casualty of Germany's unrestricted submarine warfare. On May 7, 1915, a U-boat torpedoed the British passenger liner as it sailed from New York City, New York, to Liverpool, England. The ship had fallen prey to the near-invisible underwater menace.

Two explosions followed the torpedo strike—one from the torpedo itself and a second likely caused by the ship's illegal cargo of shells and gun cotton. The *Lusitania* sank quickly. Of the 1,959 passengers on board, 1,195 died. More than 120 US civilians died in the attack.[8]

When the war began, US President Woodrow Wilson had promised to keep the United States out of the war. Many Americans supported this. But US public opinion along the East Coast and in the Midwest rapidly changed after the *Lusitania* sinking. The United States began to turn against Germany.

With another submarine threat looming, the United States learned of the Zimmerman Telegram. Germany sent the incriminating message on January 11, 1917, to its ambassador in Mexico. The telegram suggested an alliance between the two nations if the United States entered the war. Germany would then help Mexico "reconquer the lost territory in Texas, New Mexico and Arizona."[9] The threat of unrestricted warfare and the discovery of a possible alliance brewing pushed the United States over the brink. On April 6, 1917, the United States declared war on Germany, entering into the conflict just as Russia was leaving due to revolution.

It took the Lusitania just 20 minutes to sink off the coast of Ireland.

ANTISUBMARINE DEFENSES

To combat U-boats, the British planted Q-ships in the ocean. Q-ships were decoy ships disguised as defenseless merchant vessels but were actually heavily armed naval ships. Identifying these Q-ships as easy targets, German U-boats would rise to the surface to take aim with their deck guns. Once at the surface, the Q-ships would shed their camouflage and open fire on the U-boats.

Germans started recognizing British Q-ships. Only 12 U-boats were lost to the deceptive Q-ships, though 60 additional U-boats were damaged.[10]

The British also began using a new weapon called the depth charge. Depth charges were underwater bombs. Each bomb contained 300 pounds (140 kg) of explosives and a hydrostatic pistol. The hydrostatic pistol detonated after reaching a certain depth underwater.

The firing of a torpedo would give away a U-boat's location. The targeted ship could then toss a depth charge overboard, in the direction of the submarine. The depth charge generally had to detonate within 14 feet (4.3 m) of the U-boat to destroy it. However, within 28 feet (8.5 m) the depth charge could inflict serious damage on the submarine and force it to resurface, making it vulnerable to enemy gunfire.

In the first year of their use, depth charges sank two U-boats. Production increased, and by 1918 they were responsible for the demise of more than

20 U-boats. In total, depth charges sank 38 German U-boats and were at least in part responsible for the destruction of another 141.[11]

Using these antisubmarine tactics, the Allies managed to sink 24 U-boats by 1915, and another 25 the following year.[12] Despite these strategies, the German U-boat fleet continued growing. The Allies could not destroy the U-boats as fast as Germany was building them. Germany had 111 submarines in commission in February 1917, and the number swelled to 140 in October of that year.[13]

CONVOY SYSTEM

In 1917, Germany once again declared unrestricted submarine warfare, and its U-boats became increasingly

Members of the British navy recover a failed torpedo.

HYDROPHONE

During the war, ships used newly developed underwater microphones to find submerged submarines. These microphones, called hydrophones, enabled ships to listen for submarine propellers and engines. Using this device, a ship could determine the direction of an approaching submarine. However, hydrophones could not give ships more detailed information. They could detect a submarine's presence, but they could not tell how far away it was or at what depth.

aggressive. In February, the Allies lost 464,599 short tons (421,477 metric tons) of cargo to the U-boats. In April, that increased to 834,549 short tons (757,090 metric tons).[14] The British knew if they continued losing so much cargo, they would not be able to continue in the war. The Allies needed to find a solution to the U-boat crisis.

The Allies considered reinstating the convoy system, which the British previously had used for centuries. Merchant ships would sail in groups protected by an armed ship. Should any U-boats attempt to strike the merchant ships, they would find themselves vulnerable to attack from the armed ship. Merchant convoys were introduced in May 1917. While merchants had lost nearly 840,000 short tons (762,000 metric tons) to U-boats in April 1917, in November only 260,000 short tons (236,000 metric tons) were lost.[15]

THE UNITED STATES ENTERS WORLD WAR I

The United States entered the war in 1917 and the Allies had fresh resources. Approximately 2 million US soldiers were shipped to France. The Allies' convoy

The number of U-boat attacks began to decline after the United States joined the war in 1917.

was largely possible because the United States provided destroyers, which were large, fast, and maneuverable warships designed to protect other ships. The United States even helped the British with a massive mine-laying campaign in the North Sea. Called the Northern Barrage, the United States and the United Kingdom laid more than 70,000 mines to block North Sea exits. The United States laid more than half—approximately 57,000—of the mines.[16]

By 1918, the German submarine fleet began losing vessels quickly. The rate at which the Allies sank the U-boats gradually approached the rate at which they were built. The Allies destroyed 66 U-boats in 1917. The previous year, the Allies had sunk only 24 U-boats—approximately the number the Allies destroyed in just the final three months of 1917 alone. Between January and October of 1918, the Allies destroyed 88 German submarines.[17]

BRITISH SUBMARINES

The British navy also used submarines in the war. It used these underwater weapons to great effect against Ottoman forces at the battle of Gallipoli from 1915 to 1916. Other Allied warships struggled in the Dardanelles. In those hazardous straits, however, British submarines managed to attack U-boats and destroyers and slip past mines and barrage nets. One British submarine even made it to Constantinople, now Istanbul, fighting and sinking Ottoman transports, warships, and merchant ships there.

By armistice, more than half of Germany's U-boats had been destroyed. And terms in the Treaty of Versailles required Germany to give up its remaining 138 submarines. Despite these losses, the unparalleled power of submarines as weapons was evident throughout the war. This stealthy underwater menace sank 5,408 ships, sending 11 million short tons (10 million metric tons) of cargo to the bottom of the ocean.[18]

U-BOAT LOSSES IN WWI

Although U-boats experienced success at the beginning of the war, the Allies started finding ways to bring down these underwater threats. The most successful were mines laid by Allied forces during campaigns such as the Northern Barrage.

CAUSE	U-BOATS LOST
Ramming	20
Gunfire	20
Enemy Torpedo	18
Depth Charge	30
Aircraft Bomb	1
Enemy Mines	48
Unknown	19
Other	22[19]

UC5

World War I was the first war to bring combat to the skies via airplanes.

AERIAL WEAPONS

At the beginning of World War I, pilots from both the Central powers and the Allies would often greet each other as they flew past. In the air for reconnaissance, the pilots would smile and wave to pilots from warring nations. Four years later, the skies were a different scene. Gone was the friendliness among enemy pilots. Far above the scarred battlefields and muddy trenches, an entirely new kind of battle was taking place. Airplanes had brought the battles to the skies.

AERIAL RECONNAISSANCE

For decades militaries had taken to the skies in war. The French had used observational balloons for reconnaissance during both the Napoleonic Wars (1803–1815) and the Franco-Prussian War

(1870–1871). During the American Civil War (1861–1865), both sides had employed hot air balloons to keep tabs on the enemy. World War I was no different. Both the Central powers and the Allies used observation balloons to gather information on enemy movements.

Anchored to the ground, these massive balloons were filled with hydrogen. A basket hung below the balloon. From the basket, a trained observer could keep watch on enemy lines from a height of several thousand feet. A telegraph system in the gondola enabled the observer to update those on the ground with new information.

Both the Central powers and the Allies relied on airplanes for aerial reconnaissance as well. In 1903, the Wright brothers took off on their landmark flight in North Carolina. This first airplane managed to travel 120 feet (37 m) in 12 seconds of flight.[1] Eleven years later, World War I began, and airplanes were still in their infancy. These early war airplanes could reach elevations of 10,000 feet (3,000 m) and travel at approximately 50 miles per hour (80 kmh). However,

BALLOON BUSTERS

Pilots who attacked observation balloons were known as balloon busters. They had one of the most dangerous jobs in the air. The ground around observation balloons was surrounded by antiaircraft protection, and defensive airplanes were prepared to strike balloon busters. To destroy the balloon, a balloon buster had to brave these defenses—all before the balloon was pulled back down to earth. Despite the difficulty, in two weeks, US pilot Frank Luke managed to destroy more than 12 balloons.[2]

Filled with hydrogen, observational balloons were vulnerable to explosions.

they were still crude constructions. These wood-and-cloth aircraft could fly for only two to three hours. They were barely able to take off with the weight of the pilot, an observer, and the necessary fuel. The cockpits were open to the elements, and navigational technology was primitive. For reconnaissance, pilots and their aerial observers flew over enemy lines, gathering information. This information would be passed on to officers below.

At first, observers made sketches of the ground below. However, they soon recognized photographs could more easily and accurately document enemy lines, as well as changes in enemy positions and army sizes. The information gathered with these aerial cameras proved very valuable. In the spring of 1916, the Allies relied heavily on aerial photographs in the first battle of the Somme in Picardy, France. For months before the battle, observers photographed in detail the German line. Approximately 19,000 photos were taken in preparation.[3] These were pieced together to make one large, mosaic map of the German trenches.

AIRCRAFT-MOUNTED MACHINE GUNS

As aircraft continued bringing in valuable information, each side recognized their opponent was probably also collecting valuable intelligence. Therefore, pilots and observers began taking small arms up in the air with them. They brought rifles, pistols, and other handheld weapons, even slingshots, in case they encountered enemy airplanes. There was even a report in 1914 that a British airman threw his pistol at a German pilot when his gun ran out of bullets.

As the war progressed, the belligerents began attaching machine guns to their aircraft. However, with propellers at the front of the aircraft, these mounted

Many British airplanes were two-seaters, allowing for a pilot and a gunner who would fire at enemy pilots.

guns presented problems. The observer, who also became the gunner, was faced with limited gun range. Shooting straight ahead was the most effective way to strike opponents, but gunners were unable to do so for fear of striking a propeller blade.

LAFAYETTE ESCADRILLE

The United States did not enter World War I until 1917. But a group of US airmen joined the French air service earlier in the conflict. These seven men formed a small unit called the Lafayette Escadrille in 1916. After hearing word of the exploits of the Lafayette Escadrille pilots, many more US men volunteered to fly for the French. So the Lafayette Flying Corps, a larger organization, was created for all US volunteers. When the United States joined the war, these US pilots were transferred to positions with the US military.

The French tried attaching steel wedges to the propeller blades. These wedges deflected machine-gun fire that passed through the propeller. Although it allowed machine-gun fire to pass, the bullets that struck the propeller decreased the aircraft's efficiency. The first pilot to test the wedges in combat was Frenchman Roland Garros in 1915. During Garros's first run, he encountered a German airplane. He approached the aircraft head-on and fired through the propeller. The bullets struck the enemy pilot, and the German airplane fell from the sky. Garros's success with the deflectors, and his victories that followed, led one US pilot Arch Whitehouse to later claim, "Garros had given the machine gun wings."[4]

But just weeks after Garros shot down the first German airplane with the deflectors, the Germans countered the Allies' technology with new technology of their own. Anthony Fokker was a Dutch airplane builder working for the Germans. He created an even more efficient way to fire machine guns between propeller blades. His "interrupter" device used the propeller's revolution to control when the machine gun fired. The machine gun and the propeller were synchronized, and the bullets would not strike the propeller blades.

By July 1915, the Germans had equipped their airplanes, which Fokker also designed, with the device. German Lieutenant Oswald Boelcke was the first pilot to use Fokker's invention on the battlefield. On August 23, 1915, Boelcke shot down an Allied plane with the interrupter device. Boelcke would continue on to become one of Germany's early aces, earning the title "the father of air combat."[5] And Germany quickly adopted Fokker's interrupter.

HEROES IN THE SKY

A type of aerial warfare called dogfighting developed. Dogfights were chaotic battles that occurred thousands of feet in the air. During dogfights, two or more aircraft—and sometimes entire squadrons—swiftly maneuvered and battled in the sky. The pilots employed cunning tactics while trying to gain the upper hand. One young Canadian pilot described a dogfight experience:

> The enemy aircraft were coming at me from all sides, I seemed to be missing some of them by inches, there seemed to be so many of them the best thing I thought to do was to go into a tight vertical turn, hold my guns open, and spray as many as I could. The fight was at very close quarters; there seemed to be dozens of machines around me.[6]

MANFRED VON RICHTHOFEN

1892–1918

German Baron Manfred von Richthofen had more kills in World War I than any other pilot. Born to an aristocratic family in Prussia, Richthofen started as a cavalry officer in the war. In 1915, however, he leaped at the opportunity to become a pilot. He failed his first flying test. But experienced ace Oswald Boelcke eventually took Richthofen under his wing, and Richthofen was flying with Boelcke the day the veteran died.

Richthofen took great pride in each of his combat successes. After each kill, Richthofen had a silver cup engraved with the kill number, the total of victims, the type of airplane, and the date. He had to halt the practice after 60 kills because of Germany's silver shortage.

Richthofen became a national hero. His portrait was printed on flags, neckties, ashtrays, and postcards as well as in newspapers. And after shooting down four planes in one day the pilot was invited to dine with German Kaiser Wilhelm II.

In 1917, Richthofen painted his aircraft red, which earned him his nickname, the Red Baron. The Red Baron was credited with 82 kills before he was shot down in April 1918, and 13 of those came in his final month.[7]

Pilots from both sides, such as Germany's Baron Manfred von Richthofen, quickly became the heroes of the war. Civilians clamored for stories of the pilots' daring escapades. Pilots who had downed ten or more enemy aircraft earned the title ace. But pilots generally did not survive for very long. In 1917, most of them had a life expectancy of just 11 days after entering the cockpit.

ZEPPELINS

Even before the Wright brothers' first flight, German Count Ferdinand von Zeppelin found a way to fly. In 1900, Zeppelin launched a massive airship, which came to be called the Zeppelin. This behemoth in the sky was filled with lighter-than-air gas. Gondolas hung down from the airship's body, holding the pilot and crew members.

The German military recognized the military potential of Zeppelin's sky beasts. It planned to use the airships' range and bomb-carrying ability for bombings. Before World War I broke out, the navy was already building a fleet of these machines, and ten were ready when the war began. They would use the weapons to bomb the United Kingdom, hoping this would force the British from the war.

On May 31, 1915, German airship commander Peter Strasser ordered Zeppelins to bomb London for the first time. The Germans had already bombed other locations in the United Kingdom. However, those bombs had been aimed

at strategic military and industrial locations, although they also struck residential areas. The Zeppelins unloaded 3,000 pounds (1,400 kg) of bombs on the city, killing seven civilians.[8] There were ten more raids on London and the eastern coast in 1915. Although the British defenses grew stronger, they could not match the airships.

These early Zeppelins reached between 3,000 feet (900 m) and 8,000 feet (2,400 m) in altitude. At that height, they were safe from British airplanes and antiaircraft weapons. But as British defenses and airpower increased, the Zeppelins needed to fly higher and higher. Strasser had "height climbers" developed. At 700 feet (213 m) long and ten stories tall, these massive airships could fly at

Zeppelins were imposing presences in the sky.

20,000 feet (6,000 m). This altitude presented problems for the airship's crew. One airship officer commented on the unpleasantness of flying at 15,000 feet (4,500 m): "We shivered even in our heavy clothing and we breathed with such difficulty in spite of our oxygen flasks that several members of the crew became unconscious."[9] There was little oxygen so high up in the atmosphere, and the extreme height caused some to become dizzy or nauseous, or even pass out.

At the beginning of the war, Strasser believed Zeppelins would provide Germany an enormous advantage over the Allies. But the airships had many problems. At hundreds of feet long, they were difficult to miss on the horizon. They only bombed on moonless nights, but British searchlights could easily pick up their recognizable cigar shapes. The Zeppelins' navigational systems were primitive, so their crews often had to use the glow from cities, railroads, or rivers to find their targets. And they were easily blown off course in bad weather.

Zeppelins were also unknowingly designed as flying bombs. A metal structure gave shape to each Zeppelin, and within the metal structure were 19 individual balloons. Each of these balloons was filled with hydrogen. Hydrogen was lighter than air, which gave the Zeppelins lift. But it was also a highly flammable gas. The Zeppelins could easily ignite and burn, killing the crew at 10,000 feet (3,000 m). The British adapted their defenses to this. They developed special bullets meant to break through the airships' hulls, as well as incendiary bullets

BARRAGE BALLOONS

The United Kingdom used balloons as a line of defense against air raids. In 1917, the British developed barrage balloons. Balloons were positioned 10,000 feet (3,000 m) in the air, 500 feet (150 m) apart. Strung between each balloon was a horizontal cable, from which hung steel wire. This setup either forced airplanes into much higher altitudes, limiting their accuracy, or forced them to fly at predictable heights, and exposed them to a barrage of antiaircraft fire.

called flaming bullets. Together, these could pierce the Zeppelins' sides and cause it to ignite.

British defenses had improved by September 1916, and the airships' success rate began dropping. In response, the German military sent in Gotha bombers. These airplanes were designed specifically for carrying bombs. They could carry four 220-pound (100 kg) bombs on their wings. Twenty-three Gotha bombers inflicted more damage in one June 1917 raid than all of the airship bombing raids of the war. The bombers dropped 10,000 pounds (4,500 kg) of explosives, and 162 civilians died and 426 were injured. Approximately 788 people were killed and 1,844 injured in 22 Gotha raids that took place between May 1917 and May 1918. The Gothas' casualty toll was far higher than that of the Zeppelins.[10]

Despite Strasser's faith in the airships, the Zeppelins had not fared well in the war. Only seven of Germany's approximately 80 Zeppelins remained after the conflict. In total, the Zeppelins dropped approximately 6,000 bombs, twice the amount released by bombers. Five hundred and fifty people were killed, while 1,357 were wounded.[11]

COMMAND OF THE SKIES

At the start of combat, both sides were unprepared for the first aerial war. The British had 48 airplanes and the French had 136, while the Germans had 180 and the Belgians had 24.[12] However, as airplanes demonstrated their value as weapons, these numbers vastly increased. By war's end, more than 200,000 aircraft had been built by both sides.[13]

With Fokker's interrupter, the German army took control of the skies over the western front. So powerful were Fokker's airplanes that the British called them the "Fokker Menace." It took the Allies six months to respond to the interrupter with their own equivalent technology.

Throughout the war, control of the air swung between the Central powers and the Allies. Neither held airpower for very long. This scramble for dominance led to the rapid development of airplanes. One British fighter pilot wrote, "Every new machine was an experiment, obsolete in the eyes of the designer before it was completed, so feverishly and rapidly did knowledge progress."[14] Airplanes flew higher, faster, and for longer. By armistice, these air machines could sprint 150 miles an hour (240 kmh) and climb to 24,000 feet (7,300 m).[15] In a mere four years, airplanes progressed from crude fliers to killing machines.

CHEMICAL WEAPONS

On April 22, 1915, in Ypres, Belgium, the Germans released more than 188 short tons (170 metric tons) of chlorine gas from 5,000 steel canisters along their line.[1] The lethal gas drifted downwind toward the enemy, carried by the wafting easterly breeze. Allied soldiers watched from their trenches as the slow, ominous fog approached them. A soft wind pushed the greenish-yellow cloud forward, sinking into the trenches.

The soldiers could not help but breathe it in and were met with pain they had never felt before. Soldiers scratched at their throats and gasped for air. They coughed and spat blood. They cried out in pain and called for water. As one British soldier described it,

Some [soldiers] stumbled and fell, and lay writhing in the bottom of the trench, choking and gasping, whilst those following trampled over them. If ever men were raving mad with terror, these men were.[2]

The chlorine had crept in and burned their lungs. The soldiers could not fight the gas.

When the Germans approached the Allied line, they discovered death. One soldier observed,

The bodies of French soldiers were everywhere. It was unbelievable. . . . You could see where men had clawed their faces, and throats, trying to get breath. Some had shot themselves. The horses, still in the stables, cows, chickens, everything, all were dead. Everything, even the insects, were dead.[3]

The second battle of Ypres was the first time lethal gas had been successfully used as a weapon. And it left 5,000 Allied soldiers injured and another 5,000 dead.[4]

WEAPONIZING CHEMICALS

German chemist Fritz Haber played a crucial role in developing chlorine and other deadly gases for Germany. Although this was the first time deadly gas was used, it was not the first time chemical weapons were employed in the war. In 1914, the French military released grenades filled with tear gas at the battle

FRITZ HABER

1868–1934

Chemist Fritz Haber led Germany's experiments with weaponizing chemicals. His work developing and using poison gas on the battlefield earned him the nickname the "father of chemical weapons." He was the first to suggest that Germany use chlorine gas on the battlefield. Later, he was also responsible for the development of phosgene and mustard gas. Even after the war had concluded, Haber continued to research poisonous gas. Despite evidence that suggested otherwise, Haber believed chemical weapons were more humane than artillery.

Early in the 1900s, Fritz Haber developed a process that made it possible for fertilizer to be mass-produced. This fertilizer played a major role in helping feed the world's increasing population. Some believe this discovery was among the most important of the 1900s. In 1918, Haber won the Nobel Prize in Chemistry for his role in creating this process.

Born a Jew, Haber had converted to Christianity as a young man. But when the Nazis gained power, he was forced to flee. Because of his work on chemical weapons, Haber had trouble finding a new home. Scientists looked

CHEMICAL WEAPONS

GAS	YEAR FIRST USED	FIRST ARMY TO USE	EFFECTS
Tear Gas	1914	French	Burns and tears up the eyes, burns the skin, causes gagging
Chlorine	1915	German	Burns the throat and lungs, causes lungs to fill with liquid
Phosgene	1915	German	Burns the throat, causes fluid in lungs and coughing
Mustard Gas	1917	German	Burns and swells the eyes; blisters the skin; causes diarrhea, vomiting, and temporary blindness

of the Frontiers. Tear gas contained a mixture of substances that irritated the mucous membranes in the eyes, throat, mouth, and lungs. This leads to crying, coughing, difficulty breathing, and temporary blindness. However, the French used such a small amount the Germans did not feel its effects. The German army attempted to use tear gas in January 1915, releasing tear gas shells in an attack against the Russians in Poland. But extremely frigid temperatures prevented the tear gas from taking effect. Struggling to break the deadly stalemate on the western front, Germany debuted lethal gas as a new breed of weapon in 1915.

These first chemical weapons were deployed using canisters, which meant the wind needed to be just right for the gas to be swept into enemy territory. The German troops had to change the position of the canisters and postpone their use for weeks because of wind direction. The British first attempted a gas attack in September 1915 at the battle of Loos in Loos, France. The troops released 150 short tons (140 metric tons) of chlorine gas from 5,000 canisters.[5] A change in the wind direction, however, sent the gas back into the British trenches, poisoning hundreds of their own soldiers.

Both sides worked quickly to develop gas-filled shells, which were more predictable than the gas cylinders. With gas shells, soldiers could drop the poison gas directly onto enemy lines without having to rely on favorable weather. In 1917, the Allies first used the Livens Projector in battle at Arras, France. The

German Red Cross members attempt to revive soldiers who have fallen to gas bombs during battle.

projector had the ability to launch a bomb filled with 30 pounds (14 kg) of deadly phosgene gas 1,200 yards (1,100 m).

CHLORINE AND PHOSGENE

Specific characteristics made chlorine a good chemical weapon. Chlorine was inexpensive and easy to obtain in Germany. Even in frigid temperatures, it would stay a gas, and it sank into trenches because it was denser than air. Chlorine attacked victims' lungs, causing them to fill with liquid. In effect, the soldiers drowned in their own bodily fluids.

Phosgene proved to be the most deadly of the gases used in World War I. It was responsible for approximately 80 percent of poison gas deaths.[6] This colorless gas warned of its presence only with the faint smell of hay. Both the Central powers and the Allies began combining chlorine and phosgene in battle. They hoped together the two would cause more casualties.

Germany also delivered the gases in deliberately planned waves. Each wave was designed to achieve a different desired effect. First, soldiers would release a nonlethal gas, such as tear gas. This would irritate the enemies' eyes and make them vomit, prompting them to remove their gas masks. Then the Germans released a lethal gas, such as chlorine or phosgene. Without their gas masks, the enemy would be vulnerable to the deadly gas.

MUSTARD GAS

The German military introduced mustard gas, named for its distinct scent, at the third battle of Ypres, or Passchendaele, in 1917. It quickly became among the most feared of the chemical weapons. The British suffered 14,000 casualties from mustard gas within three weeks of its first use.[7] Of the war's total gas casualties, mustard gas was responsible for approximately 90 percent.[8] But few of those casualties resulted in death.

Previous chemical weapons had mostly affected the respiratory system, but mustard gas attacked the entire body. A soldier could not protect himself with a gas mask alone, because the gas also attacked people's eyes and blistered their skin. Even skin covered by clothing was vulnerable to blistering if a person was exposed long enough.

British soldiers did not realize they were being gassed when the Germans first used mustard gas. They believed the Germans were playing a trick on them, so they took off their gas masks. But mustard gas produces delayed effects. Within a few hours, the soldiers began to vomit, their eyes began to swell, and their skin started to blister.

Sometimes mustard gas also inflicted temporary blindness on soldiers. As one US doctor observed of exposed soldiers,

> By the time the gassed cases reached the casualty clearing station, the men were virtually blind and had to be led about, each man holding on to the man in front with an orderly in the lead.[9]

A particularly dangerous characteristic of mustard gas was its longevity. As mustard gas settled, it contaminated the area in which it settled. It clung to leaves, fabric, soil, and even animal hair for weeks. If the settled gas was disturbed, soldiers could be exposed to the gas again and fall victim to its effects.

GAS MASKS

During the first attack at Ypres, Allied soldiers had no gas masks to protect themselves. However, some Allied soldiers were able to quickly fashion makeshift gas masks. They dipped cloths in water or in their own urine and held them over their mouths and noses. The damp fabric acted as a filter to protect the soldiers from the gas.

It took the Allied soldiers just a few weeks to manufacture their own gas masks. The first British gas masks were crude and mostly ineffective. One soldier described them as a "piece of muslin, which we tied round the nose and mouth

Wearing gas masks to protect against chemical weapons became part of soldier training.

and around the backs of our heads."[10] Soon, however, the British developed a new, more effective mask. It was a wool hood completely covering a soldier's head. The hood had been soaked in chemicals that neutralized the effects of the gas. A small window at the front enabled the soldiers to see. The hoods provided soldiers' eyes and lungs with some protection. But these masks were also cumbersome and fragile.

By 1916, all British soldiers were issued box respirators to protect against gas attacks. These small machines weighed approximately 3.3 pounds (1.5 kg). Respirators sent air through filters, metal containers containing charcoal and chemical particles, which neutralized the poisonous gases. The box respirators protected soldiers from most chemical agents used in the war, and they were easily modified to protect against new chemicals that were introduced. But the masks could be hot and uncomfortable. One British officer observed,

RESPONSES TO THE USE OF CHEMICAL WEAPONS

After the Germans' first chlorine attack at Ypres, many condemned the use of chemical weapons. One Allied soldier described it as "the most fiendish, wicked thing I have ever seen."[11] It was called a "new form of cowardly and inhuman warfare."[12] Even German Otto Hahn, who worked closely with Fritz Haber in Germany's chemical weapons program, was uncomfortable with the use of the weapons.

However, American chemist James Conant and Haber both felt differently. Conant argued he did not understand "why tearing a man's guts out by high explosive shell is to be preferred to maiming him by attacking his lungs or skin." Haber similarly argued, "Chemical warfare is certainly no more horrible than flying pieces of steel."[13]

Even more advanced chemical weapons have made an appearance in many conflicts since World War I.

The air you breathe has been filtered of all save a few chemical substances. A man doesn't live on what passes through the filter—he merely exists. He gets the mentality of a wide-awake vegetable.[14]

As the war progressed, gas masks were also designed for dogs, horses, and messenger pigeons.

By armistice, chemists had experimented with at least 3,000 chemicals, and 50 of those had made it onto the battlefield. Approximately 124,000 short tons (112,500 metric tons) of gas had been produced.[15] Gas accounted for an estimated 1.3 million casualties, including approximately 90,000 deaths.[16]

Tanks were an effective way to break through the enemy's network of barbed wire.

TANKS

Two inventions aided in the conception and development of tanks, originally called landships. The first was the invention of the internal combustion engine at the end of the 1800s. Second was the invention of the Holt tractor. This tractor moved on continuous steel tracks instead of wheels. It could easily cross rough or uneven ground and even overcome obstacles.

TANK DEVELOPMENT

In October 1914, Colonel Ernest D. Swinton proposed the development of an armored war vehicle to the British War Office. He wanted the vehicle to "primarily be a machine-gun destroyer" and have the ability to climb over German trenches and nests of barbed wire.[1] To create this machine, he suggested they turn

ARMORED CARS

At the war's onset, luxury British carmaker Rolls-Royce provided the military with 100 armored cars. Armored cars were equipped with bulletproof bodies. Instead of continuous tracks like a tank, these vehicles had wheels like standard cars. A revolving tower, armed with a machine gun, was fixed to the top of the car. The muddy trenches of France made these cars ineffective on the western front. They were, however, successfully employed in Gallipoli in 1915, in Romania in 1916, and in the deserts of the Middle East from 1916 to 1918.

to the Holt tractor. His suggestion was largely ignored until heard by First Lord of the Admiralty Winston Churchill. Under Churchill's influence, the navy created a top-secret Landships Committee to experiment with and develop Swinton's idea.

Swinton needed the tanks to be able to cross an eight-foot- (2.4 m) wide trench and climb a five-foot- (1.5 m) high obstacle. A tank managed to pass these tests in February 1916. At 26 feet (8 m) long and 28 short tons (25 metric tons), this tank could travel on the uneven battlefield at only three miles per hour (5 kmh). It could cross a trench as wide as ten feet (3 m), and it held eight crew members.[2] This is how Swinton described the tanks:

> They are powerfully-engined armed automobiles, enclosed in a bullet-proof casing for the protection of their crews. Propelled on the caterpillar principle, they possess considerable powers of traveling over rough ground, both in crossing trenches, craters, and other cavities, and climbing over raised

obstacles, such as parapets, can tear their way without difficulty through wire entanglements, can uproot largish trees, and can throw down the walls of ordinary dwelling-houses.[3]

The British War Office ordered 150 of these early vehicles.[4]

Unaware of the United Kingdom's tank development, France began developing its own armed and armored war vehicle in 1915. France created some heavier tanks, but when they debuted in 1917, they were largely unsuccessful on the battlefield. Upon learning of the British tank in 1916, France also went to work creating a lighter tank. What it produced was the Renault. It was a 13-foot- (4 m) long tank that weighed 6.5 short tons (5.9 metric tons) and could travel more than six miles per hour (10 kmh).

CHALLENGES ON THE BATTLEFIELD

British tanks first saw battle at the first battle of the Somme on September 15, 1916. Originally, the United Kingdom had planned to use the tanks once they had amassed a large number of them. However, British general Sir Douglas Haig demanded they employ the weapons before a large number had been produced. He believed tanks would be a key weapon in the deadlock at the Somme.

The tanks' debut at the Somme was lackluster. Eighteen of the 49 tanks involved were out of commission quickly even without the help of the German army.[5] Some tanks broke down even before reaching the battle or during the

The Germans captured this British Mark IV tank.

fighting. Others could not pass over the soft ground, while large shell craters trapped other tanks because they were unable to pull themselves from these deep battlefield holes. Few tanks managed to break through German lines, but those that did saw great success.

Although the tanks were largely ineffective, Allied troops met them with joy and excitement. Laughing and cheering, British soldiers followed their new armed and armored weapons across the battlefield. German soldiers, however, met the tanks with fear. As one German soldier reported,

A man came running in from the left, shouting, "There is a crocodile crawling into our lines!" The poor wretch was off his head. He had seen a tank for the first time and had imagined this giant of a machine, rearing up and dipping down as it came, to be a monster.[6]

Though few machines broke through German lines, the appearance of just one prompted the surrender of 300 Germans.[7]

At the Somme, the tanks did not show themselves to be the dominant, war-winning weapons the United Kingdom had hoped for. But even so, one US journalist estimated the tanks had saved the lives of approximately 20,000 British soldiers at the Somme.[8] And despite their failings, Haig recognized the potential of these weapons on the battlefield. After their debut at the Somme, he ordered another 1,000 of these machines.[9]

France unleashed its first tanks during the Nivelle Offensive in northern France in April 1917. Armed with six crew members, two machine guns, and a three-inch (7.6 cm) artillery gun, these heavy tanks could travel at five miles per

INSIDE TANKS

Conditions inside the early tanks were unpleasant. On some tanks, the radiators were housed inside the vehicle. Temperatures inside the already cramped tank could rise as high as 120 degrees Fahrenheit (49°C). Heat and engine fumes sometimes caused soldiers to pass out, and crews reported that men needed to drink more than one gallon (3.8 L) of water each day when in action because of the heat. Furthermore, the racket made by the guns inside the tanks led to, as one soldier described it, "appalling" noise.[10]

Light tanks for two crew members were mass-produced in World War I.

hour (8 kmh). However, they had not been tested on the battlefield. In action, the French quickly learned they had missed a key design flaw in the machines. They had placed the gas tank at the front of the tank, but failed to give it enough armor. One hit from a shell, and the tank would ignite. The French had amassed 132 tanks to use in the Nivelle Offensive. Nineteen of those broke down, while another 57 were halted by German fire.[11]

BATTLE OF CAMBRAI

The 1917 battle of Cambrai saw the first use of the tanks as their creators had envisioned them. In this surprise attack, the British mobilized nearly 400 tanks.[12] Companies of 12 tanks, arranged in triangle formations, crawled across the gentle landscape. One hundred yards (90m) behind, infantry followed the tanks. Only a quick, heavy artillery barrage preceded the advance, leaving German soldiers caught off guard as they watched these massive beasts lumber out of the mist. By the end of the day, 12 hours later, the British had breached Germany's defensive line. They had advanced six miles (10 km) along a seven-mile (11 km) front while suffering only 4,000 casualties.[13]

The Allies ultimately lost at Cambrai, but it was not because of the tanks. If anything, the tanks emerged from the battle victorious. Almost 180 tanks were out of commission by the battle's end, but their performance had proven their power and ability on the battlefield.[14] Paul von Hindenburg later wrote,

FASCINES

The tanks at Cambrai featured a new addition: fascines. Germany began to build wider trenches after the tanks first appeared at the Somme. This made it more difficult for tanks to cross. In response to this, the British added fascines, or heavy, tightly bound bundles of brushwood, to their tanks. Fascines were carried on the tops of the tanks as they advanced. The tanks dropped the fascines into yawning German trenches, forming improvised bridges so tanks and soldiers could pass.

British tanks return via railway after the battle of Cambrai.

"The English attack at Cambrai for the first time revealed the possibilities of a great surprise attack with tanks."[15] The tanks' full potential had finally been realized.

TANKS AT WAR'S END

Germany was not immediately convinced of the utility of tanks. Its military did not begin developing the weapon until 1917. And the tank it released in October 1917 was bulky and awkward. Weighing 32 short tons (29 metric tons), it measured 26 feet (8 m) long and 10.5 feet (3.2 m) wide.

Germany produced just 20 tanks before armistice—a far cry from the 3,870 built by the French and 2,636 churned out by the British.[16] The German military did, however, recognize their usefulness after the war had ended.

WORLD WAR I IN REVIEW

Fighting on the eastern front drew to a conclusion early in 1918. Germany launched five offensives against the Allies on the western front. After defeat at the second battle of the Marne near Paris, France, in August, the momentum shifted. The Allies defeated Germany in August at the battle of Amiens in Picardy, France, and the Meuse-Argonne Offensive in September. The Allies and Central powers signed the armistice on November 11, 1918.

In this war of attrition, the Allies, boosted by the assistance of the United States, simply outlasted the Central powers. But in the process, 8.5 million soldiers died in the war. Another 21 million were wounded.[17] The number

TERMS OF SURRENDER

The terms of Germany's surrender forced the disarmament of the nation. The Allies believed this would ensure that Germany was no longer a military threat, which would prevent future war. Germany's military was severely reduced to just 100,000 soldiers.[18] The Germans had to hand over a vast amount of their weapons, including the remainder of their U-boat fleet and many naval ships. The terms also forbade Germany from producing modern arms, such as airplanes, tanks, and poison gas. The weapons they were permitted to manufacture could be produced in only a few selected factories. Germany, however, started rearmament for World War II secretly at first, but then openly when Adolf Hitler and the Nazi Party came into power in 1933.

Tanks drive through the streets during the World War I victory parade on July 14, 1919, in Paris.

of civilian casualties is equally staggering, with an estimated 13 million civilian deaths.[19] New, modern technology combined with outdated, inadequate tactics had transformed the battlefields into acres of slaughter. At the four-month First Battle of the Somme alone, both sides suffered approximately 1.2 million casualties in exchange for a total Allied gain of five miles (8 km).[20]

The world emerged from the Great War changed. Old-world strategies had no place in battle, and industry and machines ruled all. Mechanization reigned supreme. Airplanes, Zeppelins, U-boats, machine guns, and rapid-firing artillery saw widespread use for the first time. Tanks and chemical weapons had taken center stage, developed in direct response to the war's trench conditions. And these technologies continued to grow and evolve through World War II.

World War I, too, drew civilians into the war, transforming them into pawns and targets and incorporating them into strategies to end the war. With its blockade, Britain hoped to starve Germany into peace. With its unrestricted submarine warfare, Germany hoped to do the same to the UK. And with the Zeppelin blitz on London, Germany hoped it could inspire fear in the masses to prompt the United Kingdom's exit from the war. These strategic moves were repeated during World War II. Germany continued its bombing of London, while the United States itself dropped powerful, war-ending nuclear bombs on the Japanese cities of Hiroshima and Nagasaki in 1945.

Winston Churchill, who eventually became Prime Minister of the United Kingdom, later wrote,

> *The Great War through which we have passed differed from all ancient wars in the immense power of the combatants and their fearful agencies of destruction, and from all modern wars in the utter ruthlessness with which it was fought. All the horrors of the ages were brought together, and not only the armies but whole populations were thrust into the midst of them.*[21]

With World War I, the nature of war had forever changed.

TIMELINE

1884
Hiram Maxim invents the machine gun, which can fire up to 700 rounds per minute (RPM).

1903
In North Carolina, the Wright brothers achieve the first flight, traveling 120 feet (37 m) in 12 seconds in their airplane.

July 28, 1914
World War I begins.

September 1914
Both sides dig in, marking the start of trench warfare.

July 1915
Dutch inventor Anthony Fokker unveils his interrupter gear.

June 7, 1916
At the battle of Messines, British forces detonate explosives in underground tunnels.

September 15, 1916
The British debut tanks at the battle of the Somme with minimal success.

April 1917
In April, the United States enters into World War I, declaring war on Germany.

September 1914

British cruisers *Aboukir*, *Cressy*, and *Hogue* become casualties of one of the war's first U-boat attacks.

April 1915

At the second battle of Ypres in April, Germany is the first belligerent to use lethal gas as a weapon.

May 1915

A German U-boat torpedoes ocean liner *Lusitania*, killing 1,195 passengers including more than 120 Americans.

May 1915

Zeppelins unload 3,000 pounds (1,360 kg) of explosives on London in the first-ever blitz.

July 1917

Germany introduces mustard gas to the battlefield.

November 1917

The United Kingdom mobilizes approximately 400 tanks to great success at the battle of Cambrai.

March 1918

Germany's so-called Paris Guns attack Paris from 75 miles (121 km) away.

November 11, 1918

Both sides sign the armistice agreement to end World War I.

ESSENTIAL FACTS

KEY PLAYERS

- Hiram Maxim's invention of the machine gun in 1884 had a dramatic impact on how World War I was fought.

- Dutch inventor Anthony Fokker's interrupter gear allowed machine guns mounted on an airplane to fire through the propeller.

KEY STATISTICS

- By war's end, chemical weapons had caused an estimated 1.3 million casualties and 91,000 deaths.

- U-boats sent 5,408 ships and 11 million short tons (10 million metric tons) of cargo to the bottom of the ocean.

KEY WEAPONS

In September 1914, both the Central powers and the Allies carved trenches into the ground for protection from enemy fire. Machine guns and artillery were the war's greatest killers. The power of machine guns played a large part in the development of the trenches. In response to the British naval blockade, Germany declared unrestricted submarine warfare with its U-boats, torpedoing targets while hidden under the waves. Early airplanes were used for reconnaissance by both sides. As airplanes began to improve, belligerents attached machine guns to their airplanes. Germany unleashed 168 short tons (152 metric tons) of chlorine gas in 1915. Both sides began to develop stronger chemical weapons such as phosgene and mustard gas. The Allies developed the tank, an armed and armored war vehicle, specifically to fight in trench conditions. Tanks could easily drive over the barbed wire littering no-man's-land and were impervious to machine-gun fire.

IMPACT ON THE WAR

World War I saw the first widespread use of machine guns, rapid-firing artillery, and magazine-fed rifles. Trenches created a deadlock, and both sides raced to develop new technology and weapons to break through this stalemate. Machine guns could easily mow down thousands of advancing enemy soldiers, while artillery enabled belligerents to launch shells at enemy trenches. Neither side was prepared for weapons so powerful, and each vastly increased its holdings by the war's end. U-boats struck and sank ships indiscriminately, and many civilians were killed. This, in part, led to the United States entering the war. Attaching machine guns to airplanes resulted in aerial battles called dogfights. Pilots emerged from the war as heroes. Tanks were still in their infancy when the war ended but continued to be refined over the next few decades before World War II.

Necessity demanded innovation and technological development to build weapons that could break the deadlock. With World War I, the nature of war had forever changed.

QUOTE

"Soldiers rode in on horses, and they left in airplanes."

—Historian Libby O'Connell

GLOSSARY

ACE

A combat pilot who has accumulated ten or more kills.

ARMISTICE

A temporary stop of fighting by mutual agreement.

ARTILLERY

Large guns manned by a crew of operators used to shoot long distances.

BELLIGERENT

A state or nation waging war.

BLITZ

An intense or sudden military attack.

BLOCKADE

A military act in which one state uses its navy to block supplies from entering a warring nation.

CASUALTY

A person killed or injured during a war.

CIVILIAN

A person not serving in the armed forces.

CONVOY

A group that travels together for protection.

CRUISER
A fast, large military ship armed for battle.

DISARMAMENT
The handing over of an army's weapons.

FRONT
An area where a battle is taking place.

HOWITZER
A short cannon that fires shells in a high curving path.

INFANTRY
Soldiers who fight on foot; the branch of the army including these soldiers.

RECONNAISSANCE
An exploration of an area to gather information about the activity of military forces.

SHRAPNEL
Shell fragments from an exploded shell.

ADDITIONAL RESOURCES

SELECTED BIBLIOGRAPHY

Cowley, Robert, ed. *The Great War: Perspectives on the First World War.* New York: Random, 2003. Print.

Dooly, William G., Jr. *Great Weapons of World War I.* New York: Bonanza, 1969. Print.

Griffiths, William R. *The Great War.* Wayne, NJ: Avery, 1986. Print.

Hart, Peter. *The Great War: A Combat History of the First World War.* New York: Oxford, 2013. Print.

Hochschild, Adam. *To End All Wars: A Story of Loyalty and Rebellion, 1914–1918.* New York: Houghton, 2011. Print.

FURTHER READINGS

Freedman, Russell. *The War to End All Wars: World War I.* Boston: Clarion, 2010. Print.

Grant, R. G. *World War I: The Definitive Visual History, from Sarajevo to Versailles.* New York: DK, 2014. Print.

Woodward, David R. *World War I Almanac.* New York: Facts on File, 2009. Print.

WEBSITES

To learn more about Essential Library of World War I, visit **booklinks.abdopublishing.com**. These links are routinely monitored and updated to provide the most current information available.

PLACES TO VISIT

Imperial War Museum, London
Lambeth Road
London SE1 6HZ
United Kingdom
+44 (0)20-7416-5000
http://www.iwm.org.uk/
The United Kingdom's Imperial War Museums are dedicated to providing information about armed conflicts, including the British role in them. Its website not only provides information specifically about the United Kingdom in World War I but also offers a podcast series devoted to bringing voices of World War I soldiers to life.

National World War I Museum at Liberty Memorial
100 W. Twenty-Sixth Street
Kansas City, MO 64108
816-888-8100
https://theworldwar.org/
This national museum is devoted to interpreting, analyzing, documenting, and retelling the stories of the First World War.

SOURCE NOTES

CHAPTER 1. THE BATTLE OF CAMBRAI

1. William G. Dooly Jr. *Great Weapons of World War I*. New York: Bonanza, 1969. Print. 55, 141.

2. Robert Woollcombe. *The First Tank Battle: Cambrai 1917*. London: Arthur Barker, 1967. Print. 42, 44.

3. Ibid. 18.

4. Peter Hart. *The Great War: A Combat History of the First World War*. New York: Oxford, 2013. Print. 370–371.

5. William G. Dooly Jr. *Great Weapons of World War I*. New York: Bonanza, 1969. Print. Intro.

6. Robert Cowley. *The Great War*. New York: Random, 2003. Print. 97.

7. Peter Hart. *The Great War: A Combat History of the First World War*. New York: Oxford, 2013. Print. 50.

8. Ernest Dunlop Swinton. *The "Tanks."* New York: George H. Doran, 1918. Print. 19.

9. "Tech Developments of World War I Video." *History. com*. A&E, 2015. Web. 3 Aug. 2015.

10. Harriet Torry. "Trench Foot." *Wall Street Journal*. WSJ, 2015. Web. 8 May 2015.

11. "The Trenches: Symbol of the Stalemate." *PBS*. PBS, n.d. Web. 3 Aug. 2015.

12. Adam Hochschild. *To End All Wars*. New York: Houghton Mifflin, 2011. Print. 136.

CHAPTER 2. MODERN WEAPONS

1. William G. Dooly Jr. *Great Weapons of World War I*. New York: Bonanza, 1969. Print. 107.

2. Ibid. 84–85.

3. Ibid. 84.

4. John L. Lienhard. "Hiram Maxim." *Engines of Our Ingenuity*. University of Houston, n.d. Web. 2 May 2015.

5. Adam Hochschild. *To End All Wars*. New York: Houghton Mifflin, 2011. Print. 164–165.

6. William G. Dooly Jr. *Great Weapons of World War I*. New York: Bonanza, 1969. Print. 80.

7. Ibid. 79.

8. Ibid. 80.

9. Ibid. 80.

10. Adam Hochschild. *To End All Wars*. New York: Houghton Mifflin, 2011. Print. 199.

11. Peter Hart. *The Great War: A Combat History of the First World War*. New York: Oxford, 2013. Print. 217.

12. William G. Dooly Jr. *Great Weapons of World War I*. New York: Bonanza, 1969. Print. 141.

13. Ibid. 63.

14. Ibid. 64.

15. Stephen F. Hurst. "The Biggest Gun in the World." *Military History* 23.10 (2007): 50–53. *EBSCO*. Web. 5 May 2015. 53.

16. "Big Bertha." *Encyclopedia Britannica*. Encyclopedia Britannica, 2015. Web. 5 May. 2015.

17. Nigel Jones. "Weapons Invented in the Heat of Conflict." *Telegraph*. Telegraph, 4 Apr. 2014. Web. 5 May 2015.

18. William G. Dooly Jr. *Great Weapons of World War I*. New York: Bonanza, 1969. Print. 5.

19. Ibid. 83.

20. Spencer Tucker. *A Global Chronology of Conflict*. Santa Barbara: ABC-CLIO, 2010. Print. 1312.

21. Jeremy Black. *Introduction to Global Military History*. London: Routledge, 2013. Print. 93.

CHAPTER 3. WEAPONS IN THE TRENCHES

1. William G. Dooly Jr. *Great Weapons of World War I.* New York: Bonanza, 1969. Print. 107.

2. Ibid. 113.

3. Ibid.

4. Robert Cowley. *The Great War.* New York: Random, 2003. Print. 103.

5. Kate Clements. "Podcast 15: Trench Raids." *Voices of the First World War.* IWM, 3 Oct. 2014. Web. 2 May 2015.

6. William J. Duiker and Jackson J. Spielvogel. *The Essential World History.* Wadsworth, 2010. Print. 569–570.

7. George Coppard. *With a Machine Gun to Cambrai.* London: Cassell, 1980. Print. 82.

CHAPTER 4. WEAPONS OF SIEGE WARFARE

1. William G. Dooly, Jr. *Great Weapons of World War I.* New York: Bonanza, 1969. Print. 97.

2. Ibid. 104.

3. Jonathan Ferguson. "The Blanch-Chevallier Discharger." *Arms & Armour* 11.2 (2014): 187–199. *EBSCO.* Web. 8 May 2015. 190.

4. Evan Hadingham. "The Hidden World of the Great War." *National Geographic* 226.2 (2014): 116–129. *EBSCO.* Web. 4 May 2015.

5. "This Day in History: Battle of Messines Ridge." *History Channel.* History Channel, n.d. Web. 5 May 2015.

6. "The Battle of Messines 1917." *Australian Army History Unit.* Australian Army, 18 Mar. 2015. Web. 3 Aug. 2015.

7. "Saturday July 1st 1916." *Lochnagar Crater.* Lochnagar Crater Memorial, n.d. Web. 5 May 2015.

CHAPTER 5. U-BOATS

1. Otto Weddigen. "Lieut. Otto Weddigen's Account of the U-9 Submarine Attack." *Lieut. Otto Weddigen's Account of the U-9 Submarine Attack* (2009): 1. *EBSCO.* Web. 26 Apr. 2015.

2. Ibid.

3. Jordan Golson. "How WWI's U-Boats Launched the Age of Unrestricted Warfare." *Wired.* Condé Nast, 22 Sept. 2014. Web. 3 Aug. 2015.

4. Stephan Wilkinson. "Killer U-Boats." *Military History* 27.3 (2010): 26–34. *EBSCO.* Web. 26 Apr. 2015. 31.

5. Louise Bruton. "The War at Sea." *British Library.* British Library, n.d. Web. 3 Aug. 2015.

6. William G. Dooly Jr. *Great Weapons of World War I.* New York: Bonanza, 1969. Print. 300.

7. Ibid.

8. Robert Cowley. *The Great War.* New York: Random, 2003. Print. 92.

9. Peter Hart. *The Great War: A Combat History of the First World War.* New York: Oxford, 2013. Print. 309.

10. David Greentree. *Q Ship vs. U-Boat: 1914–1918.* Oxford: Osprey, 2014. *Google Book Search.* Web. 3 Aug. 2015.

11. Christopher Lawton "Depth Charges." *Wall Street Journal.* Wall Street Journal, 2014. Web. 25 Apr. 2015.

SOURCE NOTES
CONTINUED

12. William G. Dooly Jr. *Great Weapons of World War I*. New York: Bonanza, 1969. Print. 308.

13. Ibid.

14. Peter Hart. *The Great War: A Combat History of the First World War*. New York: Oxford, 2013. Print. 308.

15. William G. Dooly Jr. *Great Weapons of World War I*. New York: Bonanza, 1969. Print. 308.

16. Ibid. 309.

17. Ibid. 311.

18. Stephan Wilkinson. "Killer U-Boats." *Military History* 27.3 (2010): 26–34. *EBSCO*. Web. 26 Apr. 2015. 31.

19. J. David Perkins. "German Submarines from All Causes during World War I." *WWI Archive*. WWI Archive. 10 Sept. 1999. Web. 27 Apr. 2015.

CHAPTER 6. AERIAL WEAPONS

1. Arthur George Renstrom. "Wilbur and Orville Wright." *NASA*. NASA, 2003. Web. 27 Apr. 2015.

2. William G. Dooly Jr. *Great Weapons of World War I*. New York: Bonanza, 1969. Print. 193.

3. Alan Wakefield. "A Bird's-Eye View of the Battlefield." *Telegraph*. Telegraph, 4 Apr. 2014. Web. 23 Apr. 2015.

4. Gavin Mortimer. "Giving the Machine Gun Wings." *Aviation History* 23.6 (2013): 50–55. *EBSCO*. Web. 23 Apr. 2015. 50.

5. Robert Cowley. *The Great War*. New York: Random, 2003. Print. 257.

6. Peter Hart. *The Great War: A Combat History of the First World War*. New York: Oxford, 2013. Print. 434.

7. Robert Cowley. *The Great War*. New York: Random, 2003. Print. 281.

8. Michael Duffy. "Bombers: Germany, Zeppelins." *First World War.com*. Michael Duffy, 2009. Web. 3 Aug. 2015.

9. Nicholas Nirgiotis. "Midnight Raiders." *Air and Space Magazine*. Smithsonian, Jan. 2006. Web. 3 Aug. 2015.

10. William G. Dooly Jr. *Great Weapons of World War I*. New York: Bonanza, 1969. Print. 209.

11. Ibid. 183.

12. "American Air Service Observation in World War I." *Internet Archive*. Internet Archive, n.d. Web. 3 Aug. 2015.

13. Blaine Pardoe. "Frank Luke Jr.: A Dauntless Spirit." *Air Power History* 56.3 (2009): 4–13. *EBSCO*. Web. 23 Apr. 2015. 8.

14. Peter Garrison. "What the Red Baron Never Knew." *Air and Space Magazine*. Smithsonian, Jan. 2008. Web. 20 Apr. 2015.

15. William G. Dooly Jr. *Great Weapons of World War I*. New York: Bonanza, 1969. Print. 173.

CHAPTER 7. CHEMICAL WEAPONS

1. Gerard J. Fitzgerald. "Chemical Warfare and Medical Response during World War I." *APHA*. APHA, n.d. Web. 3 Aug. 2015.

2. Peter Hart. *The Great War: A Combat History of the First World War*. New York: Oxford, 2013. Print. 142.

3. "First-hand Accounts of the First Chlorine Gas Attack." *C&EN*. C&EN, 2015. Web. 2 Aug. 2015.

4. *100 Years of WWI*. History Channel. A&E, 2014. DVD.

5. "The Battle of Loos Begins." *History.com*. A&E, n.d. Web. 3 Aug. 2015.

6. "Chemical Weapon." *Encyclopedia Britannica*. Encyclopedia Britannica, 2015. Web. 3 Aug. 2015.

7. Joel A. Vilensky. *Dew of Death: The Story of Lewisite*. Bloomington: Indiana University, 2005. Print. 14.

8. "Chemical Weapon." *Encyclopedia Britannica*. Encyclopedia Britannica, 2015. Web. 3 Aug. 2015.

9. Gerard J. Fitzgerald. "Chemical Warfare and Medical Response During WWI." *APHA.* APHA, n.d. Web. 3 Aug. 2015.

10. Ibid.

11. Ibid.

12. Peter Hart. *The Great War: A Combat History of the First World War.* New York: Oxford, 2013. Print. 141.

13. Sarah Everts. "When Chemicals Became Weapons of War." *C&EN.* C&EN, 2015. Web. 3 Aug. 2015.

14. Gerard J. Fitzgerald. "Chemical Warfare and Medical Response During WWI." *APHA.* APHA, n.d. Web. 3 Aug. 2015.

15. Ibid.

16. "Chemical Weapon." *Encyclopedia Britannica.* Encyclopedia Britannica, 2015. Web. 3 Aug. 2015.

CHAPTER 8. TANKS

1. Ernest Dunlop Swinton. *The "Tanks."* New York: George H. Doran, 1918. Print. 19.

2. William G. Dooly Jr. *Great Weapons of World War I.* New York: Bonanza, 1969. Print. 138.

3. Ernest Dunlop Swinton. *The "Tanks."* New York: George H. Doran, 1918. Print. 20.

4. William G. Dooly Jr. *Great Weapons of World War I.* New York: Bonanza, 1969. Print. 138.

5. Adam Hochschild. *To End All Wars.* New York: Houghton Mifflin, 2011. Print. 213.

6. Peter Hart. *The Great War: A Combat History of the First World War.* New York: Oxford, 2013. Print. 234.

7. William G. Dooly Jr. *Great Weapons of World War I.* New York: Bonanza, 1969. Print. 139–140.

8. Ernest Dunlop Swinton. *The "Tanks."* New York: George H. Doran, 1918. Print. 24.

9. Peter Hart. *The Great War: A Combat History of the First World War.* New York: Oxford, 2013. Print. 234.

10. Ibid. 372.

11. Ibid. 340.

12. William G. Dooly Jr. *Great Weapons of World War I.* New York: Bonanza, 1969. Print. 141.

13. Ibid.

14. Ibid. 150.

15. Ibid. 150.

16. "Tank." *Encyclopedia Britannica.* Encyclopedia Britannica, 2015. Web. 29 Mar. 2015.

17. "World War I Casualty and Death Tables." *PBS SoCal.* PBS, 2004. Web. 18 Apr. 2015.

18. "Treaty of Versailles." *Encyclopedia Britannica.* Encyclopedia Britannica, 2015. Web. 23 Sep. 2015

19. "World War I." *Encyclopedia Britannica.* Encyclopedia Britannica, 2015. Web. 3 Aug. 2015.

20. "First Battle of the Somme." *Encyclopedia Britannica.* Encyclopedia Britannica, 2015. Web. 8 May 2015.

21. Winston Churchill. *The World Crisis.* New York: Scribner's, 1923. Print. 2.

INDEX

ABOUT THE AUTHOR

Emily Rose Oachs has authored more than 30 nonfiction books for young readers in elementary, middle, and junior high school. Her recent books cover an array of topics in science and social studies, including weather, ecosystems, history, and geography. She lives and writes in Los Angeles, California.